Peeping Tom's Cabin

PEEPING TOM'S CABIN

COMIC VERSE 1928–2008
BY

X. J. KENNEDY

AMERICAN POETS CONTINUUM SERIES, No. 105

BOA EDITIONS, LTD. ROCHESTER, NY 2007

First Edition
07 08 09 10 7 6 5 4 3 2 1

Publications by BOA Editions, Ltd.—a not-for-profit corporation under section 501 (c)
(3) of the United States Internal Revenue Code—are made possible with the assistance
of grants from the Literature Program of the New York State Council on the Arts; the
Literature Program of the National Endowment for the Arts; the County of Monroe,
NY; the Lannan Foundation for support of the Lannan Translations Selection Series;
the Sonia Raiziss Giop Charitable Foundation; the Mary S. Mulligan Charitable Trust;
the Rochester Area Community Foundation; the Arts & Cultural Council for Greater
Rochester; the Steeple-Jack Fund; the Elizabeth F. Cheney Foundation; the Chesonis Fam-
ily Foundation; the Ames-Amzalak Memorial Trust in memory of Henry Ames, Semon
Amzalak and Dan Amzalak; and contributions from many individuals nationwide.

Cover Design: Geri McCormick
Cover Art: "Woman and Pears" by Lynne Feldman
Interior Design and Composition: Richard Foerster
BOA Logo: Mirko

Library of Congress Cataloging-in-Publication Data

Kennedy, X. J.
  Peeping Tom's cabin : comic verse, 1928–2008 / by X. J. Kennedy. — 1st ed.
    p. cm. — (American poets continuum series ; no. 105)
  ISBN 978-1-929918-95-9 — ISBN 978-1-929918-96-6 (pbk.)
  I. Title.

PS3521.E563P44 2007
811'.54—dc22

                    2007007950

BOA Editions, Ltd.
Nora A. Jones, Executive Director/Publisher
Thom Ward, Editor/Production
Peter Conners, Editor/Marketing
Glenn William, BOA Board Chair
A. Poulin, Jr., President & Founder (1938–1996)
250 North Goodman Street, Suite 306
Rochester, NY 14607
www.boaeditions.org

NATIONAL
ENDOWMENT
FOR THE ARTS

State of the Arts

NYSCA

To
John Mella
and to the memory of
Robert Wallace
the best friends light verse has had

Contents

6. Tawdry bawdry

7. Leftover parts

The Furnace of Life

sort of an introduction

Some of you critical consumers out there may be wondering why this book took from 1928 to 2008 to write.

Admittedly, that's a pretty inclusive sweep of time. True, I wasn't born until 1929 and didn't print any verse till 1956; but like the ancient Chinese, I reckon that your age begins at the moment of your conception, almost a year before you emerged. Right away, a fertilized egg starts gestating poems. It just hangs there, piling up material that won't see print in a hurry. Like all true artists, it can't be rushed.

Come to think of it, millions of incipient American poets must have been aborted before they ever printed a line. That can't be totally bad. At least, the country has escaped utter deforestation. As for 2008, a year that at this writing we haven't come to yet, I don't expect to write any more comic verse until 2009, if that soon. Isn't everybody, including you and me, entitled to a vacation?

My earliest bit of comic verse came out in *The New Yorker* in 1956, written when I was a white-hat sailor stationed in Norfolk, Virginia. The magazine's poetry editor, Howard Moss, must have liked sailors. Over the years, I've written a lot more of such trivial stuff, but have never understood how you tell light verse from poetry, exactly. Like hens that gulp iron nails, some poems have plenty of weight rattling around in them; yet, light on their feet, they skitter about, turn a back-flip, and make us laugh. Marvell's "To His Coy Mistress" always cracks me up, as do Donne's "The Flea" and Yeats's "John Kinsella's Lament for Mrs. Mary Moore." Such comic masterworks drive one to ponder unanswerable questions, like what is poetry, who is God, and what are we doing here.

Nor do attempts to define "light verse" get anywhere either. The term suggests negligible froth, like the pitiful head you get on light beer. For the sake of clarity I call funny things that rhyme and scan "comic verse." Maybe some are heavy enough to call poems. I hope that's all right with you.

The present book doesn't include any of my verse for children. The "Ghastly Brats" here included are new, and weren't in any of three volumes about little snots who get their comeuppances: *Brats* (1986), *Fresh Brats* (1990) and *Drat These Brats!* (1993). Those were nominally children's books, but these more ghoulish items seem better suited to an older, nastier audience. Nor do the contents of this book overlap at all with *In a Prominent Bar in Secaucus: New & Selected Poems 1955–2007* (Johns Hopkins University Press, 2007), although some people might think a few things in that book risible. If you happen to know my old stuff and don't find what you're looking for here, kindly give it a try.

Like all versifiers who have hung around for a while, I've committed things that ought to have stayed in the womb, probably. But in selecting work of the past, I have tried to take the advice of one of America's all-time favorite poets, the late, sainted Edgar A. Guest:

> *Sacred and sweet is the joy that must come*
> *From the furnace of life when you've poured off the scum.*

So here is what lurked below the scum. May it bring you a smidgen of joy, if only secular.

—X. J. Kennedy

1. People & other critters

The Poetry Mafia

Hey, Davey, boy, this here's The Brotherhood.
    Some little crud in Maine, Augustus Hecht,
    Sent you an ode you're going to reject.
You heard me. Never mind the thing is good.
You might accept it? Get your head straight, bub.
    We'd know, you know. His mailman's one of us.
    The last poem-sniffer kept a piece by Gus
Gargled a lake, his feet stuck in a tub.

But listen, our man Lou-the-Lines Montale
    Has more hot stuff than Potlatch's got lumber
        And got his family kiss straight from The Muse
(His closest rivals took sick in an alley),
    He's FAXing you—so save him space next number—
    A free-verse villanelle you don't refuse.

The Slime Eel, Also Called Hagfish

In mud the slime eel likes to lurk.
He has no eyes, he dwells in murk.
He sneaks in through a fish's mouth
Or else some entrance farther south,
Sets up his home, affixes snout,
And eats his host from inside out.
While that unwelcome guest grows fatter
The poor fish wonders, "What's the matter?
Why do I have this hollow feeling?"
To me this eel sounds unappealing
As he could be, yet someone loves him:
Koreans. They think highly of him.
To purchase him they stand in queues,
Invite him to their barbecues,
And wolf him down with eager yelpings,
Heaping their plates with second helpings.

Medical Types of Personality

The germs of housemaid's knee do not infect
Low grovelers who basely genuflect.

Mainly the grasping, miserly, and mean
Succumb to cancer of the endocrine,

While Good Samaritan and Cheerful Giver
Are hotbeds for cirrhosis of the liver.

After Scripture

(First Kings 1:2)

When doddering David
    Lacked for heat
He leapt in bed
    Between two sweet
Young concubines
    Like thermostats
And soon regained
    His old begats.

A Backward Glance

As birds stand still whose tails boys touch with salt,
Lot's wife looked back, hard-minded to a fault,
And upright as a pillar met her Maker.
Lot took a spoonful, capped her in a shaker.

Domestic Crisis

"Mother! Father! Hurry, hurry!
Something mammoth, fat and furry
Just jumped out of a banana!
It's making off with Adrianna!"

"Hmmmm," says Mother, "is it handsome?
Does it not demand a ransom?"
Says Father, "Drat the filthy brute!
One never knows what's in fresh fruit."

The Fatted Calf Views
the Prodigal Son's Return

His old man spills his water jugs for joy—
"My younger son! He's seen the light!" Aw shit,
Reason he's home to roost awhile, this boy,
Is spending-money and three squares. Throat slit,

Drained dry, my guts uncoiled like package twine,
I'll roast to feed this tramp
Who in four years of college couldn't learn
Which way to stick a stamp.

Will he reform him to a solid yup
Like poppa wants? When lizards change their spots.
Just watch the bastard wipe his mouth and romp
Back to his old fleshpots.

So listen, kiddos—learn these simple tricks.
Don't let a hammer knock you out half-grown.
Count calories and go on hunger strikes.
Shake beanstalk butts, be walking stacks of bone.

Uncle Ool Proclaims a Parable

Pounding the bar in Mickey's Liffeyside,
    Ool made all but the TV set fall still.
Hands over shuffleboard hung petrified
    While hoisting high and struggling not to spill

His foam-domed glass, he bellowed, "See this fizz?"
    Siddown, somebody yelled, *you damned old souse!*
"The human race, the head on draft beer is!"
    A low guffaw loped houndlike through the house.

"But what's below the suds line? What's it called
    That rides us suckers on its golden breast,
And us all bubbles?" —*Ool*, another bawled,
    Gas with your ass, man, give your mouth a rest.

Fluorescent lightning prowled each outraged face.
    The pitcher shuddering in his fist, Ool poured
A second glass, blew off the human race,
    And drank deep of the fullness of the Lord.

Sisyphus, or, The Writer's Lot

Sisyphus
Sisyphus
trundling your stone
up that steep mountain slope,
mud sliding down,
why work so hard, baby,
rolling that rock?
Get it up top and it
only rolls back.

"Yeah, but it's steady work.
I'm my own boss."

Sisyphus
Sisyphus
gathers no moss.

Reunion

Impassive, to a tuba chord,
 Faces like blurry photostats,
Enter the class of '34
 In wheelchairs, coned with paper hats.

Discreet, between the first Scotch punch
 And the last tot of buttered rum,
President Till works over each,
 Fomenting his new stadium.

Fire in his eyes, the class tycoon,
 Four hog-hairs bristling from his chin,
Into his neighbor's Sonotone
 Confides his plan to corner tin.

His waitress with a piercing squeal
 Wrestles a buttock from his grip.
Dropping the napkins a good deal,
 She titters, puddling oxtail soup.

Now all, cranked high, shrill voices raise
 To quaver strains of purple hills
In Alma Mater's book of days.
 Some dim subdean picks up the bills,

One last car door slam breaks a whine
 Solicitous of someone's health,
And softly through the mezzanine
 The night revives with punctual stealth.

Eavesdroppings

(a nosegay of found verse overheard in public places)

1   I thought I had it in the bag
Until she threw a crying jag.

2   Some cold I got,
and I need a cold
like I need a hole in the head
full of snot.

3   You heard about Murray?
"No. What about?"
He went out without
the truss you're not aspost
to go out without.

4   Barney you called?
No wonder you got stuck.
That guy could fuck
Up a two-car funeral.

5   Catch that witch.
"Which witch?"
That witch.
Eating the whole wheat sandwich.

Two Sour Views

1 *Speculating Woman*

Left in the lurch, I found the will
To bed down with a dollar bill
And soon forgot love's brief alarms
In Grover Cleveland's rustling arms.
A constant six percent more fond
I grew in that new marriage bond
And every new year thanked the Lord
For fresh increase and well-chaired board.

Unlike grown daughters, dividends
Make no pretense to be your friends
Nor ever give you cause to doubt
Whose hands they're in when they go out.
What mortal husband do you know
Whose interest each month will grow?
See, women, how those mates of yours
Depreciate. While mine endures.

2 An Aged Wino's Counsel to a Young Man on the Brink of Marriage

A two-quart virgin on my lap,
With hands that shook I peeled her cap
And filched a kiss that warmed me so,
I raised my right hand, swore I do,
And merged our fleshes, I and she,
In mutual indignity.

Now when I hear of wives that freeze,
Bitter of lip with icebound knees,
Who'll play high-card for social bets
And lose, and feed you fish croquettes,
Who'll nap all day and yak all night
What Ruth told Min—now who was right?—
Who'll count with glee your falling hairs
But brood a week on one of theirs,
Who'll see your parkerhouse poke out
Before they take a stitch, who pout
At change of moon, as I hear tell,
I say, son, wed you half so well.

Three Epitaphs

For a Postal Clerk

Here lies wrapped up tight in sod
Henry Harkins c/o God.
On the day of Resurrection
May be opened for inspection.

For a Rail Traveler

Here lie Jonah Jones's uncoupled remains:
A cowcatcher caught him as he changed trains.
His fragments took off in a few directions.
May he rise at the last trump to make connections.

For a Washer of Dishes

Here rattle about in the suds of the grave
The porcelain bones of a deep-sink slave.
Impeccable platters were what he wrought
With a face like a rag wrung dry of thought.
Let the scouring rain and the sponging worm
Deliver his spirit from crust and crumb
And stack him up high beyond sin and stain
In the light of the Lord to let him drain.

Early April Rattles Professor Oglebock

The clog from your limp foot
Drops with a squat *plock*—
Your sole's white flounder hoists
Five pink shrimps.

Turn down the thermostat!
Deep-freeze the comforter!
Disband the seminar
On the neoclassical temper!

Temptress, I long to roll you and your loam
Up and down busily with a water-filled drum.
One crook of your little fishtail smites my lore
Relevant as an elephant's-foot umbrella stand.

Oust irony! Pluck irony green cresses!
Let's whirl with the verdant Public Garden's
Romantic nymphs in diaphanous nightdresses
After the worsted Augustans.

The Mouthless Moth

Who'd be a male
Cecropia moth?
Short-lived and frail,
He's got no mouth.
One hour he flies—
No time to sup
Before Death cries,
"Your number's up!"

If I were in
That poor bug's shoes
And had like him
No time to lose
Until—kaput,
I'd make one last
Request: a gut-
Busting repast:
Shrimp, T-bone rare,
Champagne and, yes,
An aperture
For its ingress.

A Penitent Guiseppe Belli Enters Heaven

Wincing, the throneside angels heard him whine,
"Father, forgive me those infernal sonnets
Wherein I told how monsignori dine
On whores' hair pies and lust for bishops' bonnets.
Forgive my libels: Luke dead drunk on wine,
Martha shaking a dust mop, blest Bellini
Wiping that hole where candles never shine,
The Holy Father himself with sticking-out weenie—"

But God said, "Eh, Guiseppe, up off of your knees.
Who you think made the grape that pickled Luke?
Who built the Holy Poppa so he gets a bone
Like any man? You pray like a rotten cheese.
Beat your breast for your sins, but you got to atone
For giving my Romans a gut laugh? Don't make-a me puke."

The Self Exposed

On the Bangor-bound platform, the crowd became one
Shaping lips to me: *Now, sweet, now!*—
On the handle of my zipper, my hand dragged down,
Out it budded, my golden bough

In that plate-glass proscenium my Pullman room.
An old biddy guffawed, a valise
Being handed up to a conductor's hand
Fell, blossomed underwear—*Police!*

Came a yell. Off we lurched. What gets into me?
I'm not one to be peter-proud,
But my bird-out-of-hand longs to take its stand
On the far side from what's allowed.

People with their foreheads like income-tax forms
Make me want to throw up. I yearn
To scribble with my dibble on their neat, ruled norms.
They'll nail me yet. I never learn.

Oh, I've been to psychiatrist and priest,
I've read an uplifting book,
But it's cold and I hunger to walk forth dressed
In the quilt of the world's warm look.

At the Body Club

Before they'll transubstantiate
Our weakling muscles, ounce by ounce,
The membership admissions squad
Evaluates our bank accounts

And whiffing profit, soon conducts
A guided tour: Behold our Club
From tennis court to swimming pool
And massage room—ay, there's the rub.

One earnest convert to the faith,
Hard pressed to shed his beer gut, Gus
The lonely votary pumps iron,
Enchambered in his Nautilus

And Clee, who hates to dust or clean—
"So many steps!"—now unawares
Of irony, treads a machine
That feeds her feet unending stairs.

Dazed Al, who didn't think he could
Swat bag so long nor swim so far,
Indulgently rewards himself
With doubles in the singles bar.

A social hour Sunday night,
Discussion group on AIDS research—
Strange how in these hard-headed times
The body club replaces church,

Its slim aerobic specialists
Ordained as priests. For want of fresh
Godheads, we genuflect within
Temples we raise to our own flesh.

2. Songs & a ballad

Song: Hello, Dali

Hello, Dali,
Well hello, Dali,
It's so nice to see your Mona Lisa smile
Through her moustache, Dali,
At the cash, Dali,
You keep stashin'
From Christ's passion
Painted Dali style.

So drape them tree crotches
With them limp watches!
Other fellas may wax jealous—
They're just flops, pops!
Holy gee, Dali,
Obvious to me, Dali,
At rakin' in the bacon you're the tops.

Flagellant's Song

When I was young,
Stud-jackass hung,
    A lecher by persuasion,
Each girl who stirred
My nesting bird,
    I'd rise to her occasion,

But now that snow
Upon my brow
    Has fluttered down and perched,
I can't address
Moist loins unless
    My backside's smartly birched.

So whip away!
Flail, flog, and flay!
    Hooray! the birch-bark's thwacking!
Its whistling wood
Incites my mood
    And soon I'm hot attacking.

When men get old
Desire grows mold
    And wives turn cold and thoughtful—
Then, tender words
Are for the birds.
    They'll give good wives a gutful,

But flail and lash
Inspire men's flesh
    As oats and hay, racehorses.
If more wives flayed
They'd be well laid
    And rare would be divorces.

I dreamed a sight
Of Sade last night,
    Alive like you and me.
"Your grace," said I,
"How did you die?"
    In little bits, said he.

More Foolish Things Remind Me of You

with apologies to songwriter Eric Maschwitz

Theses on archetypes in rapsters' lyrics,
Menus describing hash in panegyrics,
    Cheap vases aping Mings—
    Pretentious things
        Remind me of you.
Loud slurping noises from the next apartment,
A critic's lecture on what Hitler's art meant,
    Dead snakes the tomcat brings—
    Disquieting things
        Remind me of you.

You came, swell dame, swooped down on me.
Like Visigoths you looted me,
You burnt me down, then booted me.

Lines sliced to little bits by deconstruction,
Loose gobs of fat removed by liposuction,
    Toys after children's play—
    Sheer disarray
        Reminds me of you.
A sculped Discobolus with penis missing,
Forgotten novelists, Surtees or Gissing,
    Leftovers growing mold—
    Everything old
        Reminds me of you.

By God, how odd to call to mind
Those tortures that you tried on me,
How, least of all, you lied to me.

Cheeseburgers gussied up with shrimps and chili,
Victorian bathers' gowns, a gilded lily,
    Hands weighted down with rings—

Overdressed things
    Remind me of you.
Fallacious arguments, a dozen doughnuts,
Car windows shot to hell when policemen go nuts,
    Suburban lawns with moles,
    Things full of holes
       Remind me of you.

Blues for Oedipus

Oracle figured
    You'd come a cropper,
       Kingdom-killin
          Mammyjammin
    Poppa-bopper!

Gods dished you the shit
    Like you deserves—
       Now yo eyeballs
       Danglin
    From dey optic nerves.

Death and Transfiguration

I was reading John Crowe Ransom
When two tits poked through the transom
    And a voice hissed, "Pssst! will either of these do?"
"I am not," said I, "selective."
But a snooping house detective
    Hauled off both, with what intent I never knew.

While I washed in extreme unction
Both my lobes forgot to function
    And the enzymes of decay came charging through,
Then the Angel of Destruction
Gave his trumpet liposuction
    And a summons to the Day of Judgment blew.

There before the bar of Judgment
All my pleas seemed merely fudgement
    And the lawyer to defend me failed to show.
Though with lips puffed prim and pursy
I prayed, "O Lord, grant me mercy,"
    Soon an elevator whisked me down below.

Now all day I ford a river
Of flamed cognac in a flivver—
    Thirsty work. They give me molten lead to quaff
And I frequently feel queasy,
For the living's less than easy,
    And at moments find it difficult to laugh.

American Songbag

Nostalgic Air

to the tune of "Put on Your Old Gray Bonnet"

Trot out your old Victrola
And that crunchy granola
And we'll slap Shinola on our shoes
And slip some crook payola
For some Nehi Cola
Laced with homemade bootleg booze.

Marching Song of the Men of Sodom

Oh, send those peachy kewpies forth!
Such stuff we haven't seen in weeks,
Such licky locks of angel fuzz!
Such lispy lips! Such tweaky cheeks!

Discard's Blues

I don't know why I broke down and believed you,
You swore I'd be your princess on a throne.
I never got no crown but just your scepter.
You ran away and left me all alone.

There's just three kinds of ring you gave me, honey—
A ring to say you're coming, on the phone,
A mess of fast-food onion rings for dinner,
And a brown ring round my bathtub now you're gone.

Uncle Ool's Renunciation
of the Ill-paid Trade of Verse

In ancient Greece
When men chased fleece
    And girls wore golden panties,
Bard Orpheus
Ran smack across
    A pack of crazed Bacchantes.
Torn limb from limb
They soon had him—
    By Christ, it was disarming!
For woman least
Of any beast
    Gives in to music's charming.

When Mother Church
Preened on her perch
    Above the Middle Ages,
No hunchbacked serf
That dredged hard turf
    Dared strike for living wages.
Below the salt,
On tap like malt,
    The lean-eyed bard sat anchored,
Biding his time
To bawl his rhyme
    Through tankard's clink on tankard.

Some poets dwell
In a prison cell,
    Rage ravening their hearts,
Some die of gouts
As laureates
    Or commissars of arts.
But who'd sit late

To beat his pate
     Against stone walls of meter?
He's underpaid
Who plies that trade.
     Good drink, I say, tastes sweeter.

As dogs delight
To bark and bite
     And bees to buzz an orchard,
Old oily whales
To thrash their tails
     And martyrs to be tortured,
In barroom booth
To tell the truth
     It is my solemn pleasure
As night grows late
To concentrate
     On emptying a measure.

Ah, we ourselves
Lead stone-blind wolves
     On leashes lifetime-long,
Their seeing eyes,
But they'll catch wise
     When our bones start smelling strong.
Brown beer! Brown beer!
To last all here
     Till the toothless mutts lap mush!
To die from rhyme
Or drink takes time—
     Sit down, now, what's your rush?

Darwinian Apocrypha

song to be twanged on a ukulele

Where did Cain
Find him a wife?
Was she human?
Not on your life.
    Wing-a-ling-ding-dang!
    He didn't give a dang,
    He got him some orangutan poontang.

Chorus:

Orangutan poontang,
Orangutan poontang!
Heredity, go hang!
    The whole dang dad-blamed human gang
    Started in the jungle with a monkey bang.

Billie and Stan: a ballad of the West

Now Billie La Belle
Liked to raise pure hell—
    She was beautiful, mean and hard;
Santa Barbara Stan
Was a gambling man
    With his hair slicked back with lard.

In his personal jet
Stan set out to get
    To a wide-open cowpoke town
Where the prostitute's smile
Was a turning stile
    And the shot sheriffs tumbled down.

In a mansion of sin
Stan was sipping his gin
    Straight up in a dirty glass
When across the floor
Strode a net-stockinged whore,
    Bosom golden and bare as brass.

Well, Stan gave her a slow
Slit-eyed head-to-toe
    Like he'd look for a marked card's speck,
Then concupiscence surged
And the two of them merged
    Like the halves of a shuffled deck.

In a two-room flat
With no welcome mat
    They reveled in Paradise
Till one day Billie found
On Stan, the hound,
    A garter of Nelly Bligh's.

She shrieked, full of fight,
And that sad night
    As Stan lay in bed jay-bare,
Billie swung with a full
Quart, stove in his skull,
    And left Four Roses in his hair.

With unstoppable drip
Did his heart's blood slip
    As slow as the pall we bore,
And the jury they passed
In and out as fast
    As twelve flies on a swinging door.

To grim San Quent
Guilty Billie was sent
    To scrub crappers on hands and knees,
But she puckered red lips
And wriggled her hips
    And she soon was the warden's squeeze.

Some nights when the owl
Hoots and jackals howl,
    You can hear on the lonesome range
The click of high heels
And roulette wheels
    And the jingle of new-mown change.

3. Ghastly brats

Ghastly Brats

At the market Philbert Spicer
Peered into the cold-cut slicer—
Whiz! That wicked slicer sped
Back and forth across his head,
Quickly shaving—what a shock!—
Fifty chips off Phil's old block,
Stopping just above the eyebrows.
Phil's not one of them there highbrows.

Where the dump truck left its load
Of crushed stone to build a road,
Ab and Og, those oafish twins,
Rolled and romped with foolish grins,
Somersaulting in hot tar.
No one now knows where they are,
But, recalling as we drive
How they used to be alive,
In our throats we feel a lump
Every time we hit a bump.

Mom in bed with friend Ed screwing,
Trading sips from one martini,
Didn't notice Meg undoing
The stopper, pouring in a teeny
Seething drop of prussic acid.
Ed died screaming, "Little bassid!"

Roscoe in the petting zoo
Rubbed wee creatures' backs with poo,
Smearing lambs that kiddies pet
To their parents' keen regret.

"Take the bench!" spat Coach. But Wal
Carved an evil voodoo doll
And kept poking, all through scrimmage,
Pins in Coach's spitting image.

Hacking on his home computer,
Crafty Aloysius Booter
Cracked an ultra-secret code,
Made the Pentagon explode,
Caused a ghastly guided missile
Down upon Spokane to whistle
And consigned to ash and feces
Planet Earth and all her species.
Al, confronted with his tappin's
Consequences, shrugged. "Shit happens."

.At Mom's dinner party Megan
All the while the guests spooned soup
Of Madame De Reine kept beggin',
"Please, Ma'am, do your loop-the-loop!
You must be real good at that—
Mom says you're a weird old bat."

Clem with climber's pick and rope
Scaled a giant telescope
And, height-dizzied, had his vomit
Taken for a brand new comet.

Dirty Percival, that's who,
Filled Dad's beer mug with shampoo,
Giving Dad himself instead
Of his beer a foaming head.

"Great Aunt's evening crème de menthe
Needs," mused Mal, "a boost in strength.
What if I should introduce
This fermented cactus juice . . .?"
Dear old Auntie, by and by
Loudly cackled, "Bung your eye!"
Casting down a letchy leer,
Swinging from the chandelier.

Auntie, plotting sweet revenge,
Hauls Mal with her to Stonehenge
Where the ancient druid priests
Drained folks' veins at pagan feasts.
But, Mal draped across an altar,
Knife raised, Auntie's fingers falter—
"Spill the little bastard's juices
And get caught? I'd be the noose's."
(How the mortal fear of hemp'll
Strike one stonelike in the temple!)

Touring Salem, why did Sid,
A shameless showoff kind of kid,
Suddenly become a broom?
He'd weeweed on a witch's tomb.

From the rack, with rope-stopped throat,
Father hangs like some old coat.
Junior runs to Mom to beg:
"Let's take Poppa down a peg!"

In the steaming hot tub Kurtz
Surreptitiously inserts
Piranhas starved till good and mean
Just to help Aunt Clo come clean.

Hearing of his Uncle Hugh's
Lust for castoff cowboy shoes,
Reuben rubbed red pepper root
Round the instep of a boot,
Planted it. Soon, cruising Hugh
Seized the bait and fell right to
Running tongue with eyes agleam
Round each juicy leather seam,
Found the instep, found the kicker—
Boots just couldn't hold their licker.

While we dazed onlookers gawk
Baby's borne off by a hawk.
Few, I bet, if any chickens
Ever give it tougher pickins.

Little Spider's Diary

Mother in a dreadful snit
Scampered down her web and bit
Pop's head off. So I and Brother
Dried our eyes and munched up Mother.

4. Takeoffs

A Visit from St. Sigmund

Freud is just an old Santa Claus.
—Margaret Mead

'Twas the night before Christmas, and all through each kid
Not an Ego was stirring, not even an Id.
The hang-ups were hung by the chimney with care
In hopes that St. Sigmund Freud soon would be there.
The children in scream class had knocked off their screams,
Letting Jungian archetypes dance through their dreams,
And Mamma with her bra off and I on her lap
Had just snuggled down when a vast thunderclap
Boomed, and from my unconscious arose such a clatter
As Baptist John's teeth made on Salome's platter.
Away from my darling I flew like a flash,
Tore straight to the bathroom, threw up, and then—*smash!*
Through the window there hurtled and bounced on the floor
A big brick—holy smoke, it was hard to ignore,
And I heard further thunder and, lo and behold,
Came a little psychiatrist eighty years old.
He drove a wheeled couch pulled by five fat psychoses
And the gleam in his eyeballs could trigger hypnosis.
Like subliminal meanings his coursers they came
And, consulting his notebook, he called them by name:
"Now Schizo, now Fetish, now Fear of Castration!
On Paranoia! On Penis-fixation!
Ach, Gott, yes, that brick through your glass I should mention:
Just a simple device to compel your attention.
You need, boy, to be in an analyst's power:
You talk, I take notes—fifty schillings an hour."
A bag full of symbols he'd slung on his back;
He looked smug as a junk-peddler laden with smack
Or a shrewd politician soliciting votes
And his chin-beard was stiff as a starched billy goat's.
Then laying one finger aside of his nose,
He chortled, "What means this? Mein Gott, I suppose

There's a meaning in fingers, in candles und wicks,
In mouseholes und doughnut holes, steeples und sticks.
You see, it's the imminent prospect of sex
That makes all us humans run round till we're wrecks,
Und each innocent infant since people began
Wants to bed with his momma und kill his old man;
So never you fear that you're sick as a swine—
Your hang-ups are every sane person's. Und mine.
Hadn't Hamlet the hots for his mom? There's the rub. .
Even Oedipus Clubfoot was one of the club.
Hmmm, that's humor unconscious." He gave me rib-pokes
And for almost an hour explained phallic jokes,
Then he sprang to his couch, to his crew gave a nod,
And away they all flew like the concept of God.
In the worst of my dreams, I can hear him shout still,
"Merry Christmas to all! In the mail comes my bill."

The Budweiser Eagle

with a deferent nod to Alfred, Lord Tennyson

He clasps each can with crooked hands
In six-packs bound with plastic bands.
Ribboned ANHEUSER-BUSCH, he stands.

The wrinkled drinker slowly hauls
Ass to the john's bescribbled stalls
And with a belch like thunder falls.

Thomas Hardy Sees Harsh Days Fall upon Wessex Agriculture

Why are they mowing so slowy, Joey,
    Hoisting their feet as though cast-iron shod?
Has inscrutable Fate downbefallen, know ye?
    "Aye, God's turned odd.

"He's reverted the year to unreeling backwards:
    Now it falls down to up, does the summer shower,
And the corn that we sow leaps perversely sackwards,
    While the kale springs up cauliflower.

"Ah, curst earth! What shall we dirtfolk do now—
    Nuzzle and crench round a glotted cup?"
In a bolt of lightning that lumines the loo now
    Booms a voice from on high: *Dry up.*

Abou Ben Ad Man

with apologies to Leigh Hunt

Abou Ben Ad Man—his kind who should need?—
Drowsy one night from Scotch and smoking weed
That screened your cancer through a moondust tip,
Dozed by his houri, let his lids unzip
To spy an angel (halo, yards and yards
Of plumes) with a gold card-sorter sorting cards.
His piece of tail had made Ben Ad Man bold
And, what the hell, no point in growing old.
He said, "Hey, angel, kid, what's that you screwin'
Around with there?" Said the angel, "Who let you in?
I'm sorting out which people are most pious."
"You got me down? I go to mosque, oh my yes!"
The angel squinched his eyes, fine print to see,
Long searched—"Can't find you for the life of me."
"OK," said Abou, fat grin on his pan,
"You tell the Prophet I'm a people fan.
I work on dames to buy designer rags.
I'll make it worth your while. You want two Jags
To tool around in? Fur coats? TV screen
Wide as your wall? Your own rigged slot machine?"
The angel scribbled, scowled, and disappeared.
Come Doomsday, Abou placed just where he'd feared:
High on the list of Allah's worst smoked kippers,
Right next to Hitler's name and Jack the Ripper's.

Three New Versions
of "Mary Had a Little Lamb"

1. *In the earlier manner of Robert Lowell*

I heard the Lamb descend on Scollay Square,
Not Back Bay, where the rattle of his jaws
Suffered the whey-faced children clicking pool
Cues to besmirch our Sabbathtide. Blue laws
Forbade, O Mary, ferrying to school
His bleating, white and pear-
Shaped body that must gallop lest the claws
Of teacher snatch him while the pallid owl
Of wisdom blink and stutter. Trappists, howl
Your miserere mingled with guffaws.

Mother of God, what fleece more white than whales'
Could rack their blubber vats? Your hickory switch
Thwacks tail and pupils. Birched raw, thunderstruck,
Lamb-fish, fish-lamb—Christ, who knows which is which?
He sells Nantucket whalers down on luck
Spumoni marinara, rum in grails,
And spurns the sweating rabble who would grease
Their griddle with his blubber. He was sure
To go where Mary went, for she was pure
And swaddled in the whaleskins of his fleece.

2. In the Manner of W. S. Merwin

In the cold hour of my setting out
alone for the place of chalk where children go
I wake in the dark and foresee
his whiteness that must cling
always to me a succubus of fleece
I sense the form of that approaching shape
that I name schoolbus then we climb
together up its steps the driver guns
the bellow of its engine and I hear
a bleating baa and soon the jeers of boys
who will not let a lamb of snow belong
here in this room where words and numbers fill
my minutes until recess but the rules
are falling to the floor in spears of ice
to shatter with a soundless noise of rain
roaring the teacher roaring in my ears

3. In the Manner of Sylvia Plath

You do not do, you do not do in school,
Lamb, wool blizzard—
Just you follow me,
I'll slice you up for chops.
Your bleeding meat will hiss
Like goosegrease in the blackface of my pan.

Don't gaze at me like Jesus, lambie pie.
You break rules, in the end you're bound to lose.
So take your pious nose out of my shoes.
You give me whim-whams, or (Herr Gott!) the blues.
It's males like you, you sheepdipped rat. J'accuse.
I've had enough. And screw you too, Ted Hughes.

Famous Poems Abbreviated

1

Of man's first disobedience and its fruit
Scripture has told. No need to follow suit.

2

Once upon a midnight dreary,
Blue and lonesome, missed my dearie.
Would I find her? Any hope?
Quoth the raven six times, "Nope."

3

Whoosh!—hear the Sea of Faith's withdrawing roar?
So, baby, let's make love tonight, not war.

4

Who will go drive with Fergus now?
You lazy cocks and cunts,
I thought I'd ask you anyhow.
Well don't all speak at once.

5

Whose woods these are I think I know.
Shall I just sack out in the snow
And freeze? Naaaa, guess I'd better go.

6

Got lost, met Virgil, took a tour of Hell
Where all the different ways that guys had sinned
Were what they got. Two caught in passion's spell,

For instance, they were whirling in a wind.
Then climbed Mount Purgatory. Lots of things
I purged me of. Met Bea again. She grinned.

Heaven was rose-shaped. Angels buzzed on wings
Like bees. The Virgin let me ogle God
And all He was was one big bunch of rings.

In retrospect, that whole damned trip seems odd.

Robert Frost Discovers
Another Road Not Taken

Two roads diverged in a wood
As though in argument.
I had to keep going on one
To get to the end of a scent
That a nostril had begun,
But I picked out the no good.

What did it lead me to?
The old moose chewing her teat.
Still I'm bound to put up with Fate
Despite that aftermath.
There has to be some kind of path
Under a body's feet.

5. Clean ones & clerihews

Literary Limericks

Trouble in Thebes

"What a booboo!" said Oedipus Rex,
"Here I've called down this horrible hex,
    Murdered Pop—that was rough—
    Married Mom—it's enough
To turn anyone sour on sex."

The Ghost's Complaint

On the ramparts at night, Hamlet's dad
Says that life after death's pretty bad
    And with Mother so quick
    To shack up with the prick
Who poured guck in his ear, he feels had.

Lear Shown the Door

Begged the ex-king, "Please, Goneril, dear,
Won't you buy my old soldiers a beer?"
    Sneered that light of his heart,
    "Why, you silly old fart,
There's the heath—get the hell out of here."

Process of Composition

Scott Fitzgerald while toiling on *Tender*
Felt continually stumped by the gender
    Of a pronoun and, hell,
      Words were bastards to spell—
So he'd knock off and go on a bender.

Another Rose for Emily

Old Miss Emily, snobbish and cranky,
Used to horse around town with a Yankee
    And on waking in bed
      With the dust of the dead
Went *kerchoo* in her delicate hankie.

The Devil's Advice to Poets

Molt that skin. Lift that face. You'll go far.
Grow like Proteus yet more bizarre.
    In perpetual throes
      Majors metamorphose—
Only minors remain who they are.

Sinister Limericks

Can Great-grandmother's mind be unsound?
Every midnight she totters around
    Voicing cries of distress
    In a dripping wet dress
That she got off of someone who drowned.

See malevolent Mrs. McCrust
Poking pins in that doll! How unjust!
    Why, it closely resembles
    Her husband, who trembles
Whenever she gives it a thrust.

As Eliza stood twanging her zither
She beheld a vast sea serpent slither,
    Oozing slime, up the beach
    Till it came within reach
And she disappeared, no one knows whither.

Lady Lil dreamt a dream to alarm her:
That a horrid ghost plotted to harm her.
    In the night it would strike
    Deadly blows of its pike.
Now she sleeps in pajamas of armor.

Ever since that witch doctor head-shrinker
Turned the top of me tiny, the stinker,
    Though I may have escaped
    Unsymmetrically shaped,
I have been no great shakes as a thinker.

When Aunt Shiela strolls forth in her shroud
Doing things that ought not be allowed,
    On a leash at her heel
    Lopes an eight-legged eel.
Oh, she always collects quite a crowd.

An imperious matron of Lynn
By no means could have possibly been,
    For she'd traveled through time
    Back to primeval slime
And sprayed Raid on her very own kin.

In a jungle brake young Abercrombie
Cried, "Oh where can my Poppa and Mom be?
    I suspect that this pot
    That I float in grows hot
And my host's a carnivorous zombie."

In the churchyard of Saint Marylebone
Dwells a person aloof and alone,
 Who sedately and palely
 Goes walking forth daily
And nightly sleeps under a stone.

Muttered Mortimer Mordant, "What if
I should loosen the lines of the skiff
 In which Aunt sits knitting
 And watch her go flitting
Straight over yon watery cliff?"

On a punishing night in White Plains
As I tightened Great-grandmother's chains,
 An intrusive sub-ghoul
 Dripped a dribble of drool
And voraciously sucked out my brains.

Said the dragon, "Excuse me, Saint George,
But you've left your sword back at the forge.
 Oh, I've never yet harmed
 Any knight who's unarmed
Until now"—and proceeded to gorge.

As I jumped into space on a bungee
Every bone in my body went spongy
    When with one abrupt spurt
    I collided with dirt.
Now I'm lying here pushing up fungi.

Celebrities

Peter Lorre
Won lasting glory
Portraying heaps
Of creeps.

    Humphrey Bogart
    Gave speeches slow, curt,
    That he'd let slip
    Past a stiff upper lip.

Oliver Hardy
Grew large and lardy
From dining to excess
On many a fine mess.

    Butterfly McQueen
    Retired from the screen
    On hearing the gripe
    "You stereotype!"

Begged Edward Lear,
"Victoria, dear,
Don't draw such grim jowls
On your owls."

    Samuel Gompers
    While still in rompers
    Went out on strike
    For a new bike.

Johnny Appleseed
Was ignobly treed
By hostile bears
Who preferred pears.

Lois Lane
Maintains her vain
Desire for sex
With a man sans specs.

Dante Alighieri
Found free verse scary
So he cast his grand schema
In terza rima.

Said Robert Burns,
"No Grecian urns
For me. Just mice
And lice."

Aimee Semple McPherson
Believed in God in one person,
So she raised a Mahal of a temple
To the glory of Aimee Semple.

Dylan Thomas
Showed early promise.
His name's no dimmer, man,
On Robert Zimmerman.

Poetic Ends

1

Hart Crane
Flushed himself down the drain
When it seemed clear
That *The Bridge* didn't cohere.

2

Charlotte Mew
Into her whisky threw
Lysol, effecting
Her disinfecting.

3

Weldon Kees
Stepped out on the breeze,
His work unrequited.
Still, he keeps being sighted.

4

Edgar A. Poe
Ought to have said "Oh-oh"
When plied with jiggers
By election riggers.

5

James Whitcomb Riley,
Once regarded highly,
Lies in literature's cellar,
Poor feller.

6

Ambrose Bierce
Penned satires fierce.
He thought it mannish
Simply to vanish.

Assorted Pentastiches

When wee David before he was throned
Stood confronting Goliath, he groaned,
    But then popped that big geezer
    A bonk on the beezer
That crumpled him, thoroughly stoned.

"Oh, go soak your head!" said Narcissus
To his image. "Some love affair *this* is!
    I find little surprise
    In your watery eyes
And your all too predictable kisses."

Before battle Ulysses S. Grant
With a stagger broke out in this rant:
    "Who the hell does Abe Lincoln
    Think he is to get stinkin'
On my stash of J. W. Dant?"

As he crouched by his couch, Sigmund Freud
Felt profoundly perplexed and annoyed—
    "Ach, these idiots snivel
    The dreadfulest drivel
And I've got to pretend it's enjoyed."

To his studio Pablo Picasso
Liked to lead little girls with a lasso
    And compel them to pose
    In inadequate clothes
While he sang a lascivious basso.

Swore Thor Heyerdahl, "Damn! my Kon Tiki
Has been growing progressively leaky.
    By the beard of Osiris,
    I'd sail in papyrus,
But a paper boat? That would look freaky."

Said a Las Vegas boss, "Listen, Twylla,
Cut the art crap. This ain't Jacob's Pilla.
    Just make sure you includes
    Lots of numbers with nudes
Dirty-dancing with Ding Dong Gorilla."

A fastidious man from Saint Paul
Couldn't stand to see anything fall:
    Every spatter of rain
    Caused him exquisite pain
And each sunset would prompt him to bawl.

Wailed an earnest young monk of Duluth,
"Where O where is the ultimate truth?"
    All at once from above
    Dropped the dump of a dove—
Prompt reply, if a little uncouth.

A lugubrious lady of Lawrence
Would regard each new day with abhorrence.
    "When I wake up," she said,
    "Just to get out of bed
Seems a good deal more work than it warrants."

Bawled a barfly, "The God's honest truth
Is that me, I'm the ghost of Babe Ruth.
    Where my last homer went's
    Over there in the gents
And this next one will break your front tooth."

"Listen, dear," said my mum, Lady Crunk,
"I was once a weird painted-head punk,
    And your real dad? Some boho
    I picked up in Soho—
Thank your stars I was stumbledown drunk."

A slippery young yup from Mount Kisco
Liked to slither about in a disco
    But the date he was with
    Kept refusing to slith
Till he'd greased her all over with Crisco.

A poet or something of Prague
Whose rhymes and rhythms were sort of vague
    Wrote a limerick
    That went on interminably
And made all who heard it say, "Ugh."

A remarkable man of Bound Brook
Likes to hang up his coat on a hook,
    But what makes him of note
    Is he keeps on his coat
While he dangles there, reading a book.

6. Tawdry bawdry

The Phallic Phoenix

elaboration on a phrase of May Swenson's

The phallic phoenix loves to fish
    And crack vaginal oysters.
Its habitat is where you wish
    Though seldom found in cloisters.

With lovers sometimes it connects,
    Flutters a while, then crashes,
And when it dies it resurrects
    Out of its own hauled ashes.

Horny Man's Song

When, strolling through the carnival,
I buy you cotton candy,
Pink sugar clouds stick to your chin.
I feel prodigious randy,
But when at last we come to dine
My high hopes hit the dust—
If you won't spare me a crumb of love
Then throw me the crust of lust.

When idling by the baker shop,
We smell hot raisin bread,
But you can't stand that risen yeast,
That raw dough's upthrust head.
For one indecent meal I'd die
Or live on, if I must—
If you won't spare me a crumb of love
Then throw me the crust of lust.

Apocryphal Note to *Moby Dick*

Had Pip the cabin boy been drowned?
Not true by half, for Queequeg found
That dim perverted little wanker
Asucking on the Pequod's anchor.

Social Barrier

The curtains of our airline coach
    Are drawn across First Class
Lest any of us peasants catch
    A glimpse of sequined ass
Cavorting in a bump-and-grind
    Before fat lavish tippers
In hot tubs sipping pink champagne
    From flight attendants' slippers.

Paying for the Groceries

In shoddy flicks that hotels charge
A fee to see (the profit's large),
Women with faces cold and mean,
All legally at least eighteen,
Squeal in fake rapture, writhe and squirm
And feign delight when spurts of sperm
Spatter their faces. What grim sex.
What solemn joy. What hard-earned checks.

The Gist of Troubadour Poetry

as it might be rendered by
Reader's Digest Condensed Books

Though soft coos
    from the dovecote
        come to my ears,
    who cares?

       She
           won't
      let me
          mount.

              Oh
              woe.

Lecherous Limericks

Naval Intelligence

Sunday evenings Rear Admiral Hess
In silk stockings and flagrant undress
    Applies cudgel and flail
    To each quivering tail
In the Bachelor Officers' Mess.

In Suspense

A well-laden maiden named Margo
Has the bustiest blouse in Key Largo
    And whenever she giggles
    It jauntily jiggles
And threatens to jettison cargo.

Metamorphosis

Muttered Fisherman Wes from Westphalia,
"How I envy a whale's genitalia!
    What low prank of the gods
    Switched my crank for a cod's
Little piddlesome paraphernalia?"

Safe Sex

Even robots whose engines need oil
Feel concupiscence bubble and boil,
 But before he starts proddin'
 The male wraps his rod in
A roll of aluminum foil.

Footnote to Medieval History

Busy mercantile bankers, the Fuggers
On their travels were frequent whore-huggers:
 Between visits to stews
 They'd dispatch red-hot news
To their old stay-at-home mother Fuggers.

A Faulkner Hero

Hardly famous for moral perfection,
Popeye couldn't erect an erection,
 So instead of his knob
 He'd use corn on the cob
As a means to express his affection.

The Elizabethan Stage

Oh, the Globe lacked for lightin' and scrimmin',
Pretty boys in wigs played all the women,
    And perhaps Willie Shakes
    Often haunted the jakes
For a morsel of anal persimmon.

Technology

What a wonderful dingus has Witter!
It leaves intimate friends all atwitter
    And when lifted erect
    Who would ever suspect
It could serve as a short-wave transmitter?

Versatility

Said a Spanish grandee named Cervantes,
"I can't stand ancient ass like my auntie's.
    I prefer to dunk tool
    In horse, donkey, or mule—
Hmmmm, I reckon I'll try Rocinante's."

Ripe Old Age

By the fireside Great-grandmother rocks,
An aluminum ball in her box,
    Enjoying the spasms
    Of constant orgasms
And knitting odd misshapen socks.

Two Views of Rhyme and Meter

1

What's meter
but the thud
    thud
    thud of an old
wire carpet-beater
fogging the air
with boredom
in dull time
and the dust,
rhyme?

2

Meter
Is the thrust rest thrust of loins and peter
And rhyme,
To come at the same time.

7. Leftover parts

Ars Poetica

The goose that laid the golden egg
Died looking up its crotch
To find out how its sphincter worked.
Would you lay well? Don't watch.

A Falling-out from Glory

How shall I ever be an elder sage,
A poet laureled and lionized in age,
Now that my mane's not white but only lost?
Who could revere an old bald-pated Frost?

Acumen

What critic could be more astute
Than T. P. Random-Carper
Who pokes his pencils up his chute
And bumps-and-grinds 'em sharper?

A Poet-critic

Swap got a wildly favorable review
Written, of course, by some kiss-ass he knew
To whose last book he'd suckled up in turn.
Better to marry, said Saint Paul, than burn.

Miss Lovingwell

At fifty-five Miss Lovingwell began
A Melville beard and turned into a man.
That change was hard, but less hard than the hell
It might have been to stay Miss Lovingwell.

An Emergency at Blarney Castle

Mother of God! By both my eyes,
The Blarney Stone has shrunk in size!
The dear old thing looks fearful sad.
Now, Bryan—there's a lovely lad—
Before the first tour of the day,
Run to the warehouse right away
And fetch us a new one, will you? Thanks.
They're hard on stones, those kissing Yanks.

Supernatural Stimulus

The Yeatses on their honeymoon
    Found married life such tedium
That wily Georgie faked a swoon
    And babbled like a medium;
And on James Merrill's growing bored
    With his companion's merits,
An old Sears Roebuck ouija board
    Raised both to higher spirits.

Here lies a moral for us all:
    When love seems unexciting
Behold the writing on the wall,
    Try automatic writing;
And if your lover you'd not drive
    To gay queen, whore, or wastrel,
That other body in your bed
    Had best be someone astral.

Style

In thigh-high yellow leather boots
Plump Saphonisba strides.
A pity that, to hide her calves,
Calves had to lose their hides.

To Someone Who Insisted
I Look Up Someone

I rang them up while touring Timbuktu,
Those bosom chums to whom you're known as "Who?"

On a Well-dressed Man Much Married

Primper, whose crease is sharper than his wit,
Tried on six wives, but found not one to fit.
Why should he wear wrong sizes all his life?
Better he let the tailor make his wife.

Postscript to an Apocalypse

After the fire and ice
    In arks to Ararats
Let Christians bring church mice;
    Mohammedans, mosque rats.

English Eats

They eat toad-in-the-hole down in Stow-on-the-Wold,
Oh, they eat it with hideous glee,
Whether fresh-made or old, whether tepid or cold,
A la mode, or dissolved in strong tea.

Lukewarm toad-in-the-hole is a load to eat whole,
For its warts tend to stick to your tongue
And you'll find, bless your soul, that cold toad-in-the-hole
Will indefinitely stopper your bung.

So take care: pinch its roll, which should feel soft as coal,
Ascertain that your toadlet is spry.
If perchance, doing dirt, it should take aim and squirt,
Quaff away. There'll be mud in your eye.

Three One-liners

Nursing Mother to Infant:

Bon appeteat!

On the Decline of Psychoanalysis

The Krafft is ebbing.

The Well-behaved Penis

stands upright and law-abiding.

Begetting Likened to a Crapshoot

Dig down in your genes,
Shake them lucky rocks,
Roll somebody new—
Clickiddy bumpbump clickiddy—

Sweet angels come and sit
On these lovin' babies.
Fine brace o' twins. Full house.
Oh oh. Snake eyes.

Then and Now

I half long for those crappy days again
    When babies used to be produced by sex
Back before women washed their hands of men
    And switched to being corporate execs.
Now, nearing forty, weary of their own
    Private Lear jets with uniformed wine-tasters,
They tap the sperm bank for a little loan,
    Inseminate themselves with turkey basters.

Those were the days of pumpkin pie and dads
    Rigging kids kites, grim days before divorce,
Of home-brought bacon, nights out with the lads,
      And moose heads goggling from the mortgaged walls.
    God was no vaguely feminine Life Force,
      But Old Pop Yahweh, hung with beard and balls.

Defending the Canon

The stooping scholars labor, hot
To keep intact the status quo:
They've proved Hawthorne a Hottentot
And Milton's Mom a Navajo.

The Cow's Vengeance

Obligingly, the mild cow lets us quaff
The milk that she'd intended for her calf,
But takes revenge: in every pint she packs
A heavy cream to trigger heart attacks.

Normalcy

Right-thinking eaters, you and I,
Sink fork first in a piece of pie
At its front point, unlike one queer
I know who entered from the rear
And, what was worse, the pie was mince.
He has been put away long since.

Nasal Reproduction

My nose is clogged with polyps.
    In order to abort
The pesky little dollops,
    I spray with Rhinocort—

But if those babes still burgeon,
    I must ask, I suppose,
Doc Smith the kindly surgeon
    To hollow out my nose.

However did my nostrils,
    I wonder as I spray,
Though never wanton wastrels
    Get in this family way?

Unsatisfactory Love Poem

Your helpless addict, come what may,
    I crave you, ruthless queen,
As bums, their tastebuds burned away,
    Still lust for Listerine.

I wish I were the Siamese Twins.
    Then, darling, all night long
I'd go on loving you in Chang
    Though fast asleep in Ong.

A Triolet on Traffic

In car commercials on TV
Cars glide through vast wide-open spaces
Past lake and canyon, glad and free.
In car commercials on TV
Congested streets we never see
Nor desperate quests for parking places.
In car commercials on TV
The world is only open spaces.

Family Reunion

Drawn round the roasting of a bird
    By duty once each year,
With first a drink and soon a third,
    They baste glazed looks of cheer.

Each spine erected in its seat,
    Each head bowed low for grace,
All wait the word to fork white meat
    In through the family face.

The Seven Deadly Virtues

Humility

Not always are they admirable, the humble
Who when shrill protest's called for merely mumble.

Chastity

Shunning forbidden fruit—peel, pulp, and juice—
The chaste may find it hard to reproduce.

Generosity

The greedy rake in dollars by the fistful;
The generous grow poorer and look wistful.

Cheer

When gloom is what you hunger for, good cheer
Is nothing but a sharp stick in the rear.

Constancy

Strict constancy is an inconstant virtue:
At times some flexibility won't hurt you.

Sobriety

A certain charm inheres in strict sobriety
Until one ventures forth into society.

Modesty

Though modesty staves off one's defloration,
It's worse than useless during copulation.

Ballad Shard

Oho quhair hae ye bin, laird Percival me sone?
O quhair hae ye bin, charmin Percy?

Land o' Goshen, Mither, I'm boogered if I know,
But I had a little drink aboot a summer ago
Wi a belle dame wha had no mercy.

Short History of Drink

The invention of distilling
Has made woman warm and willing
But mankind no more impassioned
Than limp fruit in an old-fashioned.

A Clean Sweep

Bridget plies her busy broom
In the operating room
After surgery is over
To take home little treats for Rover.

To an Unpopular Novelist

Why starve? Write Gothics, be a millionaire
Recycling mansions. Just psych out *Jane Eyre*,
Make governesses scamper for their lives
Before the screams of screwloose former wives
While beetled grow the brows of lordly Byrons
At fire insurance rates in the environs.
They'll eat it up. Regale their teeth with sweets,
Supply old ghosts with passions and clean sheets
And thunders of applause will clap you, brother,
To heights undreamt of, though reviewers wuther.

River Rhymes

Down by the rancid River Rockaway
Sue got a wet foot, threw the sock away.
A trout yelled, "Don't pollute, my pretty!
They drink this stuff in Jersey City."

One day while steaming up the Amazon
I spied a maid with no pyjamas on
Doing a dance slow as molasses,
Which steamed up the Amazon. And my glasses.

Down by the scabrous Androscoggin
Clay threw a right cross to the noggin,
One functional punch like a working piston
And that was the last of Sonny Liston.
Birds sang him to sleep in a peaceful valley.
That fight was right down Muhammad's Ali.
Some called it a fix and similar jive,
For that river was where Liston took a dive.

While barging down the stinking Styx
I realized I was in a fix,
For, whisked along on hard-thrust oars,
We fast drew close to Hades' shores.
Said Charon, blind to my misgiving,
"Rowing the dead—call this a living?"

An Irish Wish Versified

Those that love us, let them love;
Those that love us not,
Let the Good Lord turn their hearts
From clam-cold to hot.

But if He won't, then let Him turn
Their ankles twisted, and cast crimps
Into their walking styles that we
May know the bastards by their limps.

Notes

"Sisyphus, or The Writer's Lot" (page 21): This item was written for a number of the *Carolina Quarterly* dedicated to Robert Watson, poet and novelist, in recognition of his having made some stones stay put.

"An Aged Wino's Counsel to a Young Man on the Brink of Marriage" (page 25): The term "parkerhouse" means a Parker House roll, with its two cheeks of dough stuck together, reminiscent of a behind.

"The Mouthless Moth" (page 28): The opening stanza is a found poem, based on "Fun Facts," an advertising comic in the Boston *Globe*, copyright 1971 by The Wrigley Company.

"A Penitent Giuseppi Belli Enters Heaven" (page 29): Beloved poet of Rome's Trastevere district, Belli (1791–1863) wrote his raunchy, anticlerical sonnets in Romanesco, not a dialect of Italian but a forebear of it. On his deathbed he begged his confessor, one Monsignor Tizzani, to burn his poems, but the wise and indulgent cleric published them. For infectious English versions, see Miller Williams, *Sonnets of Guiseppi Belli* (LSU Press, 1981); also Harold Norse, *The Roman Sonnets of G. C. Belli* (Jargon, 1960).

Song: Hello, Dali (page 35): Salvador Dali's fellow Surrealists, scrambling the letters of his name, dubbed him Avida Dollars.

Normalcy (page 102): Virginia Kidd tells me that in some parts of Pennsylvania it is considered bad luck to start eating a piece of pie at its point. Prudent souls enter from the rear.

River Rhymes (page 108): Following the orders of gamblers, Sonny Liston, heavyweight champion of the world, surrendered his title to Muhammad Ali, then known as Cassius Clay, in Lewiston, Maine, on May 25, 1965.

Acknowledgments

Some of these things come with dedications: "A Penitent Guiseppi Belli Enters Heaven" to Miller Williams; the limerick "A Spanish grandee named Cervantes" to Richard Bausch (whose own limerick on the subject inspired this one at the 1995 Sewanee Writers' Conference); and "River Rhymes" to the late William Cole.

Thanks to those editors who first printed most of these items in their periodicals: *Able Muse, Blue Unicorn, Carolina Quarterly, Cat's Ear, Classical Outlook, Cincinnati Poetry Review, The Dark Horse, The Epigrammatist, Free Lunch, Greensboro Review, Green Mountains Review, The Hampden-Sydney Poetry Review, Harper's, Iambs and Trochees, Interim, Journal of New Jersey Poets, Little Balkans Review, Massachusetts Review, Medicinal Purposes, Midwest Quarterly, New Millennium Writings, The New York Sun, The New Yorker, The New York Times Magazine, Occurrence, Open Places, brush, Poetry, Poetry NOW, The Sewanee Review, Shakespeare Bulletin, Smartish Pace, SpinDrifter, Texas Review, The Rag, The Southern California Anthology, Sou'wester, Spectrum, The Times Literary Supplement, Wittenberg Review*, and especially (because it printed an awful lot of things) *Light, the Quarterly of Light Verse.*

Some of these items were first collected in *Nude Descending a Staircase* (Doubleday), *Breaking & Entering* (Oxford University Press), *Cross Ties: Selected Poems* (University of Georgia Press), and a chapbook, *The Seven Deadly Virtues* (Scienter Press). Some first appeared in Mardy Grothe's *Never Let a Fool Kiss You or a Kiss Fool You* (Viking); Robert Wallace's *Light Year* anthologies (Bits Press, 1984–1989), and Gail White's *Kiss and Part* (Doggerel Daze). By courtesy of The Johns Hopkins University Press, four items are reprinted from two collections currently in print: "Family Reunion" and one of the "Two Sour Views" ("Speculating Woman") from *Dark Horses*; and "Then and Now" and "Horny Man's Song" from *The Lords of Misrule.*

One epigram appears in *Bartlett's Familiar Quotations*, edited by Justin Kaplan, Sixteenth and Seventeenth Editions (Little, Brown); other things, in Bernard E. Morris's *Taking Measure: the poetry and prose of X. J. Kennedy* (Susquehanna University Press). I am also grateful to anthologists who have reprinted things, among them Russell Baker (*Norton Book of Light Verse*), Gerard Benson, Judith Chernaik, and Cecily

Herbert (*Poems on the Underground*, Cassell), William Cole (*Erotic Poetry*, Random House, and *Pith and Vinegar*, Simon & Schuster), John Gross (*Oxford Book of Comic Verse*), William Harmon (*Oxford Book of American Light Verse*), Louis Kronenberger (*The Cutting Edge*, Doubleday), Louis Phillips (*Random House Treasury of Light Verse*), John Hollander (*American Wits*, Library of America), Robert McGovern and Stephen Haven (*And What Rough Beast*, Ashland Poetry Press) and Griff Rhys Jones (*The Nation's Favourite Comic Verse*, BBC Books). Profound thanks also to Richard Abcarian and Marvin Katz; Carl E. Bain, Jerome Beatty, and J. Paul Hunter; and Michael Meyer, who enshrined some of these pieces in their textbooks and called them literature.

Thom Ward, who initiated and sustained this project, made me improve several things and their titles, and supplied more than one good line of his own.

About the Author

X. J. Kennedy at age fourteen put out a magazine called *Terrifying Test-tube Tales* on a jelly-pan duplicator. Since then, he has had eight collections of poetry, beginning with *Nude Descending a Staircase* and most recently *In a Prominent Bar in Secaucus: New & Selected Poems 1955–2007*; nineteen children's books including *Brats, Exploding Gravy*, and the novel *The Owlstone Crown*; and textbooks endured by four million students. When the American Academy and Institute of Arts and Letters began its Michael Braude award for light verse, they gave it to him right off the bat. He and author Dorothy M. Kennedy live in Lexington, Massachusetts.

BOA Editions, Ltd.
American Poets Continuum Series

Colophon

Peeping Tom's Cabin: Comic Verse 1928–2008 by X. J. Kennedy is set in Monotype Bell, a digital facsimile of a typeface originally cut in 1788 by Richard Austin for the English publisher and journalist John Bell. The display font is Humana Serif, a contemporary typeface designed by Timothy Donaldson for International Typeface Corp.

The publication of this book was made possible, in part, by the special support of the following individuals:

Anonymous (6)
Peter Beren
Nancy & Alan Cameros
Gwen & Gary Conners
Susan DeWitt Davie
Peter & Sue Durant
Pete & Bev French
Dane & Judy Gordon
Kip & Deb Hale
Robin & Peter Hursh
Irvin Malin
Stanley D. McKenzie
Stephen & Marietta Payne
Boo Poulin
Steven D. Russell & Phyllis Rifkin-Russell
Deborah Ronnen
Mike & Pat Wilder
Glenn & Helen William

Printed in the USA
CPSIA information can be obtained
at www.ICGtesting.com
JSHW020138240724
66915JS00001B/1